Your Therapist Says It's Magical Thinking

Your Therapist Says It's Magical Thinking

POEMS

SADIE McCARNEY

Published by ECW Press
665 Gerrard Street East
Toronto, Ontario, Canada M4M 1Y2
416-694-3348 / info@ecwpress.com

MISFIT

Editor for the Press: Michael Holmes
Copy Editor: Emily Schultz

LIBRARY AND ARCHIVES CANADA CATALOGUING IN PUBLICATION

Title: Your therapist says it's magical thinking : poems / Sadie McCarney.

Other titles: Your therapist says it is magical thinking

Names: McCarney, Sadie, 1992- author.

Identifiers: Canadiana (print) 20220477582 | Canadiana (ebook) 20220477590

ISBN 978-1-77041-736-6 (softcover)
ISBN 978-1-77852-130-0 (PDF)
ISBN 978-1-77852-129-4 (ePub)
ISBN 978-1-77852-131-7 (Kindle)

Classification: LCC PS8625.C37436 Y68 2023 | DDC C813/.6—dc23

The publication of *Your Therapist Says It's Magical Thinking* has been generously supported by the Canada Council for the Arts and is funded in part by the Government of Canada. *Nous remercions le Conseil des arts du Canada de son soutien. Ce livre est financé en partie par le gouvernement du Canada.* We acknowledge the funding support of the Ontario Arts Council (OAC), an agency of the Government of Ontario. We also acknowledge the contribution of the Government of Ontario through the Ontario Book Publishing Tax Credit, and through Ontario Creates for the marketing of this book.

PRINTED AND BOUND IN CANADA   PRINTING: COACH HOUSE   5 4 3 2 1

For Lindsay, with thanks for all the free therapy

Table of Contents

i. Coping Strategies   1

Let It Out   2
Take Supplements   3
Turn Your OCD Rituals into Spells   4
Do Your Fucking Breathing Exercises   6
Do The Sex   7
Take Your Meds   9
Act   10
Be the Change   11
Actually Talk During Your Scheduled Talk Therapy   12
Sleep It Off   13
Don't Think about Death   14
Think about Death   16
Turn Your Pain into Art   17
Drink   18
Choose to Be Different than You Are   19
Take Comfort in Material Things   20
Revisit Your Childhood Trauma   22

ii. Surrey Girls   23

Lucinda   24
Mary Ann   28
Caroline   32
Bea   36

iii. Alternate Timelines   41

The Best Version   42
Conveniences   43
Republic 2   44

Tale of the Phoenix   46
The Cave   48
A Less Good Version   50
Negatives   51
Alt-Everything   53
Tale of the Grocer   54
A Labourer at Stonehenge   56
The Cleanse   58
Fast Food Breakfast   60
Victimology, Redux   61
The Great Reign   63
Gridlock   65
Happy   67
Tale of the Flood   68
Back, Back   69

Acknowledgements   71

i. Coping Strategies

Let It Out

Soft yet it reverberates, like static.
A hike through brambles until
even the brambles can't spy you
undone in the brush. Then, louder:

a hoarse crow's caw (which, among
the haggard Jack pines, finds a rare
acceptance). Go deeper. The canopy
of pine needles will seem to gloat

of its evergreen stability. Unpack
the sticky-zippered pup tent you bought
from Army Surplus. Sleep. Twilights:
spray for bears, jerk the unwilling

zipper around you like a straitjacket,
and Scream Like You've Found
a Severed Arm in the Woods.
Scream until it's your severed arm.

Scream until you are those woods.

Take Supplements

A supplement helps what
you're already doing, like
a glossy tear-out poster
stapled inside a magazine.

Take 5-hydroxytryptophan
(see, "tryptophan," it's just
like Thanksgiving!), proven
to boost your serotonin, or

GABA, which may be linked
to mood and sleep. St. John's
Wort is a big deal — a natural
antidepressant (serotonin!) —

while Bach Flower Remedies
contain impressions of flowers
trapped in alcohol, which aids
anxiety. A supplement helps

what you're already doing, but
these are *natural*, they can't
really hurt you. No matter what.
Why not throw in passionflower,

wild lettuce, lemon balm? It'll keep
you calm and, therefore, alive.
You've done well for yourself,
today. All together, that's $239.65.

Turn Your OCD Rituals into Spells

Your therapist says it's magical
thinking, so you drive for miles
under sun-splintered sky and flick
the windshield wipers on, off, on,

thirty times. This is your rain dance.
Now the crops may grow. You burn
incense and eat exactly half your
Cheerios as an offering to the

Corn Mother, so she will fill your life
with plenty. Check your temperature.
The old Book of Shadows that lives
in your head says to click the latch

on the bathroom door fourteen times
in rapid succession. This is as good
as sage at house-blessing, and better
than rose quartz for attracting love.

To curse someone, arrange all
the clothing you own in groups of four.
The Book of Shadows in your mind
says this will make the person barren.

Check your temperature. Pray to
the Goddess of Corn. Arrange all
your other possessions in groups
of four too, and chant so the demon

that's *really* doing the chanting finally
leaves you alone. Light four candles.
Click the bathroom latch. Magical
thinking is only for the serious witch.

Do Your Fucking Breathing Exercises

You haven't been practising the breathing
I showed you — caught, as you say, between

two panic attacks like two water buckets
you must balance on your head precisely

so that one doesn't dump and drench you.
I have had enough of your excuses like that.

The only person who can save you is you.
My studies as a sports psychology grad

student give me the authority to say: it's your
fault your anxiety isn't getting any better, OK?

You need to practice, breath in, count, breath
out, count, breath in again. You're too amped

up to do this, precisely *because you haven't
done this*. So don't whine that it's hard for you.

Just *work*. I can always tell when you're not
really trying, like a runner who chokes in the last

quarter mile. No, I know you're not a runner.
It's a metaphor, OK? A metaphor is . . . just suck

it up and do your fucking breathing exercises
and come back next week changed and whole.

Do The Sex

You're trapped in Maine in an Edward
Hopper painting: desolate, clean lines

and women all waiting for something.
The woman in bed with you awaits

something too, but giving her that
is too far-off and boring. So you talk.

And talk. You chatter your way through
each failed attempt at her coming,

ask her what she wants for breakfast
next morning even though she never

eats breakfast. You express the wish
for females to be born with pie between

their legs, instead of this dense growth
that bleeds sometimes and other times

reeks of sweetbreads. You talk so much
she begs you to stop. When you're "done"

(or she's given up), she asks you what she
can do for *you* and you lie to her. You lie

and lie down and faux-moan in gasps
of community theatre pleasure, *yes*. This

is as composed as any Edward Hopper.
You think of it in sharp angles, stark colours.

Take Your Meds

When you pour kerosene on a dumpster fire, you don't get to call it an oil lamp. Sorry. The herbal sedatives you've been popping like Pez and the serotonin-jacking supplements you paired them with wrecked you. I know you say corporate pharmaceuticals are unnatural. But is it natural not to sleep for four days? Is it natural to be stuck in a claustrophobic nesting doll (society-community-hospital-self), each layer tightening its death grip on your psyche, all ending in the unopenable centre: your delusions? I understand that you believe God willed this. I do. So have one of these. Sure, it's a communion wafer. An atypical, rapid-release communion wafer. Some water for the dumpster fire in your head.

Act

So you got a bladder problem,
or what? You're always running
offstage mid-rehearsal, but we
need you to run through these
lines. Are you memorizing every
scritch of bathroom-stall graffiti?
No? I thought not. I see you wipe
your eyes on your costume coming
back. So it's all in your head.
                                    Great!
The sly and wonderful trick of acting
is this: you get to wear someone else's
head for the night. Maybe he's a drunk
or she's a felon, but they're not all
tensed up teary in the john. So try
to run through these lines, just once.
And whenever you're ready to bolt,
think of *being* — that drunk, that felon,
that star, that *someone*. Think of this
moment, deep breaths. Think of me.

Be the Change

Give up dairy because it enslaves the cows.
Read Alan Watts out loud, how the cosmos
is one thing playing hide-and-seek with itself.
Shear all your hair like a summer sheep,
and scrawl subversive, gender-fluid graffiti

in the bathroom stalls of your workaday high
school. Clutter street corners with signs
against the current war. Take part in larger
protests too, where minute human flecks shout
up at skyscrapers filled with stoic bankers.

Stoically scold your mum for idling outside
the Walmart you vow to never enter again.
Wear hiking boots painted with the word "injustice"
so that you can stomp it out everywhere.
And when Alan Watts starts to read like bullshit,

when Walmart has a sale on hiking boots, remember
that most Zen of things: impermanence. Eat that
first illicit bite of gouda with the permission of your
oft-annoyed family, of the cosmos, and of all
the stoic bankers and lowing cows of the world.

Actually Talk During Your Scheduled Talk Therapy

Sit there long enough and I'll manage
to do it. It'll be riptide relief for you
to tell me your irregular, sopping-mess
secrets. So *tell me*. I'll bet you're cut
up over something, sometime, feeling
like dregs of piss-warm tea in a Styrofoam
cup at an AA meeting. Ever been to AA?
Ever needed to go? No. You don't need
bottles when you're a bottling plant. So
what's inside you? I want to pluck
your story from you, like the thrum
of a staccato violin. Or wrest it from you,
a treasured heirloom of some dark thing
shunted down the generations. But first,
just *TALK* . . .
      Okay. Let's start over. Are we
getting somewhere? Maybe? Maybe?

Sleep It Off

Maybe the dream where you
rent a house with your high
school BFF's cokehead aunt

(and the house, with its squadron
of Royal Doulton figurines and
brown velvet chesterfield, looks

just like your grandma's but *can't
be*), where you share a deep-body
hug with your BFF's cuddly dude

cousin and a pounding hangover
of peace besets you for three
waking days thereafter — maybe

that dream will at last undo you.
Or, you'll REM sleep for those
three nights and dream of that

brown velvet chesterfield room,
the all-girls' birthday your grandma
once threw you there. Scavenger

hunts. "Hot Potato." Wants. You'll
wake to the all-girls' scavenger hunt
of your body, your life, your brain.

Don't Think about Death

Think about red lipstick on a white paper cup,

or a moraine of pebbles left on a beach by kids
who'll never meet again. Think *I was here* scrawled
in a girls' bathroom stall, the ugly-cry breakup
aftermaths there. Think literal hearts, that pump
literal blood like your body's own Mass Turnpike.

Think pigeon feathers in festering city wind,

and pigeon poop on a diversity of windshields:
Ferraris, Hondas, everybody. Think comfortably
average fireworks displays. No, more than think:
stain a white cup bright red with your lipstick.
Kick a sandcastle back down into glass-dust.

Think, then do: sort through things with a plurality

of pieces — a box of chewed-up old building blocks,
a room — and then go in and mess them up again
with sharp angles, clogged sinks, humanism. Break
up with someone good, to get the mascara effect
of those ugly-cry tears. Think of not-mercy, mercy, not.

Think. Do. In your mind's eye, organize your childhood

freezer, circa age ten. Your family Oscar pool in a baggie.
Ignore the canned orange juice concentrate, the blocks
of cheese bread they always got on sale, the freezer-
burnt green beans you all vowed you'd eat. Someday.

Wrest out each wizened pea you used for ice packs.

Dig too far, to the cramped and crystalline corners,

and find the Ziploc body bag: frosted-over, orange-gold,
once-shimmering fins. The goldfish. Your parents gave
him to you as a reward for a good report card. You were five.
Mum, mostly, cleaned the algae, fed him. The old-fridge
Freon gives him convincing rigor mortis. Don't think

about death. Oh, God. Don't think —

Think about Death

as a bellows of breathing, in-out,
in-out: bestowing life too, like
the breath of life God gave
our dusty ancestors.

I've watched hospice patients
as a parish ministry, and in
the end the breathing always
quits them. But God and Jesus

don't quit you like a cigar.
They stay. You say you don't
deserve to live. But there is no
"deserving" gifts, unless

you want me to take it all back —
the fringed scarf I got you
for Christmas, everything.
It's like a picnic with enough

watermelon for everyone,
but some schmuck insists
on keeping only the rinds
for himself. You are that

schmuck. You'll die. No pretending.
But take this pamphlet — I know
it'll help — and try to catch
the life while it's breathing.

Turn Your Pain into Art

Abandon all hang-ups, ye who enter here!

Welcome to Art Group. Don't eat that sponge, but don't
feel boxed in by walls, by the confines of canvas or clay. Feel
free to colour entirely new lines, glue fresh hostas to your
elaborate collage and call it a new leaf. Knit, with closely
monitored needles. Watch as your most dearly held *pain*
becomes *paint*, as the government wiretaps that worry you
hourly become a snarled sculpture of plaster, real wires. Dare
to *create* when your own cranium doesn't even let you *be*,
most days. Your illnesses are like this brush I'm holding —
see the blobs of strokes when I start? But as I swish around
this page, the paint gets so thin the brush runs dry.

Drink

. . . okay, maybe not in the mouldy-
bright dorm room morning, before
you head out for mess hall breakfast,
tipsy and grinning at your oatmeal,
your toast. Not good. Do not tipple
vodka to cope with dining crowds.
And maybe not gin post-breakup,
either — all the juniper berries in all
the world will not make her re-love
you like a thrift store treasure. But
to loosen the ever-tightening bolts
of your psyche-machine? Drink. It's
never ideal, but archaeologists find
wine in so many cultures. *They* coped.
So you can cope too. Pour yourself
a smidgen of scotch, or a whiff of prime
rosé. Everything will mute to the remotest
hint of its badness, like watching it on-
screen. Or, barring all of that, get high.

Choose to Be Different than You Are

Stop! Listen to me: I am a doctor.
I see you sob over your uneaten
queso blanco. This panic attack
you keep hold of is your brain's

bad strategy to metabolize hurt.
You can reroute this pathway
in a finger snap. You can be
the cowgirl, or the rodeo clown.

Up to you. But I am a doctor
who treats hundreds of people
a year for your symptoms. You
can will yourself out of this well

you're trapped in. It's documented:
they decide not to be crazy. It's like
they flip a switch between victor and
victim. Or, they succeed as clowns.

Please think about it: no more doctors
and pills and prayers. Only you, only
your fault the treatment's not working.
You have to put in the effort. Try. Really,

try. I'd blame you entirely for your not
getting better. After all, I have many
years of expertise: as an inpatient,
as an orderly, as a doctor, as a clown.

Take Comfort in Material Things

So you weren't pretty enough to be
a ladybug in the preschool pageant,
or even a crocus or daffodil. So what?

Now, when your homeroom friends
aren't allowed in for lunch, revel in
the mystery of black plastic trash bags.

How many are there, and what second-
hand pants o'erspill them? And who
lives in the boxes and boxes of books?

The always-unreachable Christmas tree,
with its garland of dust, means you always
celebrate Something. Play with the worn-

out badminton rackets you're too much
of a klutz for, their hopeful birdie. Play with
your Game of Life missing half the people.

Consider a picnic basket pregnant with red
yarn and your dad's off-white false teeth
impressions. What's in *that* trash bag?

Who's inside of *those* boxes? Embrace
the freezerful of mace-like chestnuts,
the hutch desk's glut of pinkish memos

you wrote yourself. Two ten-gallon drums
of "candle-making" beeswax (entombing

hundreds of noble bee-corpses) guard

the front door like library lions. This library
has secrets: the '80s *Joy of Sex* you found
where everything has far too much hair . . .

Put that down and grab a stack of Polaroids
from "Out West," suburban Ontario, places
your family lived before you were here. But

you *are* here. You add your eight-year-old scrawl
to another half-pink While You Were Out slip,
try on old clothes from the black plastic bags.

In one you find a ghost costume dyed yellow,
with a Bristol-board-and-glitter-glue headdress,
from the pageant where you got to play the Sun.

Revisit Your Childhood Trauma

like a chintzy, tourist-trap town. When you disembark from
the gaudy tourist bus, you'll find you've already bought
the requisite hat and T-shirt with your pain, and that the
slogans emblazoned on each of them say so. Get lost, like
you always do, on a self-guided walking tour through Your
Trauma, end up in the part not demarcated for tourists. It's
full of an unplaceable bitterness, factory-fumigated air, and
identical, tchotchke-crammed apartment buildings. Go back
as far as you can, to the outskirts by the train tracks of your
seldom-travelled subconscious. Find the forlorn, mangy pit
bull chained up outside the woebegone trailer of your heart.
You'll want to give the dog a hug, but she's rabid and if you
close in for one she'll bite your nose off. See, that bite is
crucial to your understanding of —

that's all the time we have for this week. See my receptionist
on your way out.

ii. Surrey Girls

*Based on the photographs of Dr. Hugh Welch Diamond, a psychi-
atrist and pioneering photographer at England's Surrey County
Asylum in the mid-1800s, who believed photography had a role to
play in mentally ill patients' treatment.*

Lucinda

1.

It seems I'm to be held in this hotel forever, on this sauna bench in this slipshod health spa. It's given me the worst kind of leg cramps. Don't you have them too? Like knives and a cudgel in my calves. The cramps aren't even the worst bit. I need to speak with my tour manager, the one you and the other hotel guests keep calling Mrs. Nurse. You all call everyone that — don't they use people's names in the hungry, backwoods muck you were sired in? Well, *don't they*?! Ah, yes, hello, Mrs. Nurse. I'd like very much to leave the benches. What do you mean, "I'm sick and I'm staying"? Is that why the tour stopped? Why we're still stuck in this crumbling, ruined hotel? I suppose I'll have to stay here, then. Let myself be cramped.

2.

I used to model for the painted postcards that soldiers kept
folded in front pockets of coats. They weren't much for
clothes, them — a lace negligee, a costume pearl necklace to
cover (and yet uncover) the good gents' fervent imaginings.
Yes, I was broke and beautiful in London, broke but not
broken-up. Costume pearls. Not like the real ones I have on
now, fastened round my — what? Where did they go, my
wondrous baubles? Who's taken them, pawned them, cooked
them in a barbaric batch of freshwater pearl and diamond
stew? Spa-goers, harlots, dear Mrs. Nurse — who has eaten
my immaculate pearls?

3.

My pearls! Who has stolen or supped on my pearls? Maybe they've retreated back into their oyster, the way I shrunk back away from that fame to be cloistered in this prim hotel on these stiff wooden benches. An oyster's a good thing to catch if you're hungry. Funny hotel — we're always here, hungry. Never enough bread; must be some kind of diet. That's why someone has entirely scarfed down my pearls! I will ask Mrs. Nurse to send me food from the kitchens. Health is one thing, but I can't abide this.

4.

Mrs. Nurse — oh yes, I heard tell of the doctor. He takes glamorous pictures of all who sit here on these hard hotel benches. Well, naturally he wants to get a picture of me! Oh, what a thing, to have myself to show as a picture! But of course he'd want my old whiff of celebrity. I'll need kohl for my eyes, Mrs. Nurse, and some lipstick. No, I know the picture won't have colours — what a grand delusion! — but one always can tell if a subject's made up or if she's still at war with herself. Yes, Mrs. Nurse, I'll see the doctor. I just wish I still had my pearls . . .

Mary Ann

1.

I be middlin' today, but last night came over all dark-like about this now and this when. Each day I wait patient on the rough-on-rumps benches for something to change, unstick me from the horridsome nowness of this all. These lowdown, runagate women they've put me with — so many talk innardly so loud I can hear them, and it's clear they think there's someone here listening. Leastways all days are more the samest than the last. So I be middlin' today, take my place on our filthy pew.

2.

They brought in a new girl, her once-bonny (I be guessing) soft brown hair hacked off in the brutalist way I've seen. She were a ruddy-cheeked, picksome little thing, and it gladdened us all great to have some distraction. But the girl wouldn't take her place on the benches. She clawed the nurses with her new-clipped fingers. Then quick as sheet lightning the nurses came grabbing, bannicked and bannicked her with the rears of their hands. It wasn't no Christian sight and they'd no ought, but they bannicked her aplenty, strew behind them the homeliest welts on the girl.

3.

I be good today, but I miss awful my husband, our walks of
an eve past the church, the thick spruces. I was too much for
him, and it turns me over all guilty-like. Used to be I beleft
that if I were enough for him, it would make up for often-
times being too much. It was my moods were the problem
— I'd come over giddy and jonesing for children for weeks,
then crash like a cart horse, low in bed moaning for months
after that. He took me visiting, a new sort of doctor in the
smoke, and the doctor brought me here. So now I sit on
our slipshod pew and think on long walks once, the rustling
spruces.

4.

No, I never get visits. They said my husband's not allowed in.
But the doctor sent for me? He's truly a-coming? Well, how
tidy! But I must get tidied up, myself: it's a brittle business
looking pretty in this horrid place, with varmints skittering
dirt all up the baseboards. I want my husband, new taters all
hotted up for supper. But of course, I'll see the doctor. What
a thing, his meaning to make pictures! Say, could I nettle a
nurse for a hair comb? A time-whittled sliver of soap?

Caroline

1.

First night all the ladies-in-waiting all wait for me to hush up and finally sleep. But I close my eyes and they're vivid violent with colour: a bright nightmare, a melting hellscape of trees and meadows made from purple-orange wax. And waxworks too — a drip-faced, mechanical mock-up of Pa. I peep through my eyelids and he's still in the room, bits that grind together and lift his shabby-suited arms up this way, that. What a weird comfort, this cog-and-wax man! I tell the ladies-in-waiting I'm fretful, but they shush me up and swaddle me tight in my blanket. I have a teetering sense that I matter, that I'm marrow to somebody's bone. But what good is mattering if my ladies-in-waiting won't heed me? What's power with such a hellscape of waxworks always blocking your path?

2.

I came here in a straight-sided, hearse-looking hansom
painted, strangely, lustrous green and red with foolish-big
hummingbird wings. The footman was mean and snarl-
toothed, hardly gentle enough to be classed a gentleman.
This rough-man, then, bade me bind my arms to my sides,
and shouted me down if I thought to speak. I kept on seeing
the colours flare up from his head like fire: violets, reds.
Royal colours. The shopkeeper had happened to find me
splayed out on the floor of the Royal millinery, dressed up as
a hat-shop girl. Pa told them to take me, so they took me to
Court — here. I court, here. At Court, I am both Royal and a
Seer. That coarse, strange footman! These sour milk ladies-in-
waiting! In some other life I'd have made them all hats, had
them squint at their pretty selves in the tarnished glass.

3.

Presented at Court I find myself crowded by tarted-up
women with their own claims to the Crown. All day they
jostle each other, wearing ermine stoles and dots of bright
rouge on each cheek. They mean to take my place. I know
this as Seer. I see phantom crowns on each woman's head,
and a spectral spaniel at each foot. These won't quit barking.
I complain to the ladies-in-waiting all about this, but they
seem untroubled by the nattering dogs, and even less by
those pretenders to the Crown. I start to see the most horrid
monsters peep out from behind the ladies-in-waitings' plain
faces — with heavy brown scales, and fangs, and harsh jaun-
diced eyes. I shrink away in shock when they come to lead
me to the bath. These handsome monsters don't even look
surprised.

4.

Waxworks rub me raw in the chilly tub, cold so it doesn't melt their waxen flesh. Then I'm out and a lady-in-waiting towels me off with sandpaper, as at Court each trial tests you closer to triumph. Dr. Someone, she says (the Court photographer!) has come to take my Royal portrait. She uses different words than mine, but their meanings mingle and sound as one. If Pa could see! I close my eyes, and it's Hell there still. But I open them on the way to the picture-room, and the grimy white halls gleam like mother of pearl. In the room, he'll be prim with his flash and his black picture-box, his way of trapping and seizing whole worlds.

Bea

1.

No, Pup William. I won't be whipped — I'll tell the doctors!
You'd need hands to hold a whip to me, anyway. Say, where's
your collar? Might as well they put all of us in here collared.
They sit us up on wooden benches, Sister Prudence! I told
you on the eve! Yes'm, they sit us up on wooden benches and
barely sup us. What's to be supped upon? Hard bread and
water the colour of dying pink flowers in a lady's window
box. Yes, Pup William, I'll toss you a stick as a plaything
when they lead us out round the grounds. To sup, Sister
Prudence — why, are we to be supped upon? They ought salt
us, then, and assault us as butchers. A walk, a walk, then they
sit us up. For how long lingering? Hours. Hours, then they
march us to the shivering baths. Can't whip me there, Pup
William. I'm safe.

2.

Back from the frosted bath into too-starched linens. They plunge us in, Pup William, but the cold turns all the water to knives. May as well whip me, now; I'm already scrubbed raw. But that's right — you haven't got the fingers to whip me, nor right now the form! You're what do they call it — a ghostly apparition. A voice that spits in my ear. No, no, Pup William, that's not right! To think of Sister Prudence if she heard such language! She'd make you wipe clean your cursed tongue. They wiped us clean in the bath, all right — the water bone-cold and all of us using the same yellowed bar of tallow-lye soap. Filth for towels. Now filth from your mouth! And back we go to sit on the benches. Oh, Pup William. At least you're with me. Hello, Sister Prudence! Another spitter in my ear. Oh, Sister Prudence, the raunch things Pup William has said!

3.

Sister Prudence spits in my ear. Oh, yes, I would like to stop her spitting! What's that, Sister Prudence? No, I won't take a switch from you, won't switch to being a woman walloped. First Pup William, now you — why do you both taunt me so? Not now, Nurse. I talk to Sister Prudence now. What, Sister, made you join the cloister? A calling, a falling, what? I hear you prattle on, too, Pup William. But we are talking of Sister Prudence now. Methinks I let you both talk, I won't be hit.

Oh! I'm burnt, charred up entirely! Pup William, why has the Nurse so scalded me, with hot kettle water and no whisper of warning? Sister Prudence, would your switch have felt softer? Should I just let you do next time, the time next?

4.

The Nurses say the Doctor is coming, with a big black box to take many pictures. I don't know any photographer, Pup William, but it sounds the most wretched medical word. He comes to take pictures of us — no! We won't let him steal them. Sister Prudence, not one of the nurses will stop him! He wants to steal pictures of us, but by rights they're ours! The Nurses say the pictures are treatment. But I haven't got a cold or nothing. Pup William, I'm the fittest person. What is the ghastly photographer treating? I see. Sister Prudence, Pup William, they say I ain't got a choice. We all have our pictures taken by force, today. Say, will you come along with me, pose for the Doctor? Will both of you stay as he does what he must?

5.

The Doctor troops in with this thing called a camera. He
means to steal pictures of us! Pup William, sit. Sit with me
and don't threaten to whip me — this monstrous Doctor will
do far worse, I can smell it. Sister Prudence, has a man ever
taken your picture, taken it away from you? What if, once he
steals our picture, I can never see my face in a looking glass
again? He smiles and bids me do whatever comes natural.
He says this will help him see into me. Help him help me.
Pup William, should I bid you to whip and bite him? Sister
Prudence, should you pick up your switch? Then a great
burst of light no longer than an eyeblink — he means to
blind us all! I'll not see anything again, not just my own face.
The Doctor thanks us, turns us loose back to sit on the hard
benches. He has our image and can do as he likes. Oh Sister
Prudence, Pup William, what has the Doctor done?

iii. Alternate Timelines

The Best Version

The boy they thought would shoot up
the church had only a Nerf gun: foam-
darted the pastor and the pale-blue
pastor's wife, and split.
                        In the kitchen, you find
your mom got up early this morning,
made pralines to share with all of her
kids, baked a criss-crossed pie for you
in seven different layers of flavour. Each
one is more your favourite than the last.

Everyone understands the nuances
of identity as hopscotch, a Rubik's cube,
elementary math. As always you get
a ride to school from Jenna's Dad's
rainbow carpool unicorn, Samantha,

but today when Samantha drops you off,
you lose your grip on her slippery, many-
hued tail and hit asphalt hard, skin your
ever-nuanced knee.
                        In every timeline
there is asphalt, asphalt, and in every
one the knee-hurt is both real and unreal.

Conveniences

The stoned boys who hoot
"Whoo!" from the moving
Subaru just do it 'cause
they like the rip of wind
in their hair,
              not because she
is any combo of fat/thin/ugly/
cute. She is as irrelevant to them
as cologne, pocket squares.

She is going to buy some
Iridescent Lays™ at the corner
store and has never been fat/thin/
ugly/cute/anything.
              She got "smart"
instead, is tops in Anti-Matter Studies,
which brims over with bird classes
for burnout stoners, the kind who
hoot "Whoo!" from moving Subarus.

The corner store sign reads: Iridescent
Lays™ & Lotto, SAVE SAVE SAVE.
Save what, she thinks. *Save who?*

Republic 2

Our once-great Republic's
now confined to this airport,
where pilots pass in full airline
regalia, checking their watches
and wheeling
                  infinitesimal suitcases,
but never going anywhere. Planes
mock-arrive and never, ever take off,
and the bored-silly crew crack wise
as they eat through
                  a whole flight's
ration of cocktail peanuts, ginger
ale. The once-proud food court
Au Bon Pain has now changed
its name
                  to read Pain, Pain, Pain.
Around the perimeter of everything,
the Guardians of the Republic shove
us into meaningless queues according
to the colour
                  our souls have shone:
gold, silver, the dullest bronze. From
there we are shunted toward former
ticket counters, where they dispense
the most horrible
                  career advice. It's
a lot like horoscopes used to be, and
we'd all laugh if the Guardians weren't
packing AK-47s. For fun we hop on
the baggage carousel and go around

and around, unclaimed.
                              The Noble Lie,
of course, is that we have destinations.
Instead we pass
                      the cocktail peanuts
around and daydream what our souls
must be like, tarnished metal and weak
from spending so much time inside.

Tale of the Phoenix

Agriculture is a story they tell us
as they rock us to sleep in backs
of Winnebagos, in makeshift tents
slung o'er pickup truck beds, in
wheelbarrows they push through
bracken all night.
                          In the story
the farmers sleep in things called
a "bed," in things called "houses." Cows
and sheep sleep in a "barn," a cow-
house. Phoenixes don't
                                   sleep anywhere
at all because in this story they never
existed. Ma and Pa drive the RV all
day and night, pausing at rest stops
to refuel and meet up with other nomads,
trade cowrie shells we found on the beach
for other nomad groups'
                                   superior flatbreads,
maybe moonshine. But Ma and Pa don't
tell us about that. Instead we get the fairy
story of the farmer and his cows, how he
squeezed them for milk.
                                   Sometimes we spy
pigs, being driven in a great steel armada
of campers and even those sleek silver
Airstreams (even nomads have our "have-
nots" and "haves"). But mostly we catch
wild phoenix to eat. It's gamey, but it goes
down all right.

In a story we tell each other
but not Ma and Pa, a wicked nomad girl
is banished from her caravan because
she started a garden at a rest stop, thought
a farm was a good idea.
In the wild the girl
turned into a phoenix, and her Ma and Pa
ate her, not knowing the story. We whisper
this tale in trucks, in campers, but always,
always in the dark.

The Cave

Be careful, child — it's too loud
out there. Stay in our home-
cave until it's day-bright out
and quiet.
           Stay here and we'll
swaddle your body in furs
from our journeys out far-ward,
from animals that
                  yowled so,
desperate decibels louder
than we could stand, until
finally they died and silence
enveloped them
               like their furs
envelop us now. The loudest
we can ever hurt. Don't go out
there, child — too many noises
for our sensitive ears.
                 Better
to hunt in day-beam: bluebirds
are noisy, yes, but background
noise we've learned to tolerate.
Our species is
           newborn, fails
to make sense of what offspring
of yours, millennia down the line,
will come to call
           our sensory data.

You ask how we can stand it,

the brightness of day over stab-
sounding night? It's because
humans are
                moth-like, even as we
hunt with our hands: we're always
drawn truthward, into the light.

A Less Good Version

The world is always a little
bit worse: a couple more
car crashes every quarter,
the grocery store oranges
a shade closer to yellow.
                        These
squat brick brutes we all call
schools teach nothing but Trig
and Mourning Rituals, in which
there are scholarships if you study
harder than the Kid Who Sits
Next to You in Trig and never
strips off her windbreaker.
                        Oh,
the wind. It's hurricane-force
and gets worse all the time.
Last year the Kid Who Used
to Sit Next to You in Trig blew
away across the blacktop.
                        He
was never seen at school again,
and the Mourning Rituals class
did a service. White lilies all over
to make the living sneeze.
                        When
the living sneeze they want vitamin
C and a lot of sleep. The vehicles
keep crashing as the kids in Trig
eat yellow-orange oranges, sniffle-
cry at their empty rinds of desks.

Negatives

All the bad things we think of
come true. At age eight, you worried
your family cockapoo, Marvin,
would die as collateral damage
in a gunfight,
                              (you were precocious
then) and wouldn't you know
a gaggle of gang members moved
into that mouldering bungalow
next door?
                    Lately I've been worried
about oceans, so climate change
is all my fault, the melting of ice caps
into glacial soup.
                              Have no fear. Really.
Please have no fear. The collection
of plate-sized tarantulas
                                        living under
your bed do not help you to solve
the arachnophobia that caused them.
If you think of something neutral,
like Christmas trees turning purple,
nothing happens.
                              Avoid thoughts
of house fires, getting fired, drought,
gout, heart attacks, and the cancer
WebMD will actually give you.
                                        Hope,
and remember that being scared
TV puppets will murder you actively

51

makes puppets on TV plot murder.

But trying not to think bad things,
it turns out, is worse. Like trying
to stare past
                the light at the eye
doctor's, or willing yourself to sleep.
You just think worse things, like
another holocaust, global famine,
making you long for the scurrying
family of spiders.
                        Please, just stay still
and don't try to think of anything at all.

Alt-Everything

They've suspended elections. Instead
the candidates play different versions
of Whac-A-Mole at a county fair that
is at once the same as and completely
different from the quilt shows and cotton
candy I grew up with.
                                    In one version, the mole
never shows while you're looking. In another,
a whole family of moles peeks out, then breaks
free of its cardboard-and-plastic apparatus
to conga-line around for the president-elect.

In my favourite one, the moles play dead
and we get a term where two presidents
or prime ministers or czars have to figure
out how to govern together.
                                    One of them
buys pink-red cotton candy, the other one
buys blue, and they each throw some in
the other's mouth, hopeful. The rule of
Whac-A-Mole is, always and forever, true.

Tale of the Grocer

Babies, let me tell you: before
we roasted this squirrel rotisserie-
style, shivering, smack in the centre
of Golden Gate Park,
                        long before we
scavenged in parks at all, when I was
still a young and decent woman, babies,
let me tell you:
                        they were called groceries.
Grocery stores. Pyramids of foreign fruits —
tangelos and persimmons, and pomegranates,
whose seeds' red juice stained our teeth
like vampires'.
                        Don't fret, babies, there were
no vampires. Keep the fire nice and even on
the juicy squirrel's back.
                        Once out back behind
the local grocer the apprentice butcher taught
me the gradations of pain.
                        After I was no longer
a decent woman. So I gathered up crystals
and a gris-gris bag to curse him. Maybe it
worked. Maybe too well.
                        Maybe my curse
is what cracked their hulking grocery hulls.
Or maybe some inevitable plummet in
the economic charts on TVs in pawn
shop windows.
                        Eh? Yes, eat, babies. Relish
the squirrel in your mouth, because this

world is a vampire suckling us daily. Enjoy it,
because tomorrow, in ten minutes, who knows?

A Labourer at Stonehenge

In thousands of years, girls
who reek of patchouli will strip
off their bras
          beneath cotton-
hemp T-shirts (that amazing
woman-bra magic trick!)
at a giant rock
          festival not far
away. They will know this place
as a legend, a great sigh.
                    But
this is our giant rock festival,
now. We heave
          the neat-hewn
stone with our sinew as the druid
foreman threatens us
          with spells.
Later, they'll romanticize this time.
I know because a crone cursed
my family with foresight,
          but also
because, given enough years past,
all times are writ romantic. All.
          I took
the job because I needed money.
"Stonehenge," as all will call this
place, is the druids'
          municipal make-
work project. They won't even tell us
what the stones are *for*,

though in X
thousand years there will be many
theories. What I do know
                              is: they'll find
human bones here, claim it's a sacred
burial site. But, crone-cursed, I know:

some of that bone will be mine.

The Cleanse

The only thing anyone eats
anymore are the cinnamon-
turmeric detox capsules sold
by a tumour that mutated
from Amway.
                   All of our teeth
are lemon yellow and our pee
comes freely because we still
drink water (distilled and not
from the tap, you moron:
chlorine is poison,
                   don't you
study the pamphlets that paper
each bus stop, each doctor's
office where they only prescribe
more turmeric pills?
                   Don't you?)
The crinkle-skinned nursing
home crowd can still recount
the secret pleasures of eating:
take one cookie
                   from the cookie
jar and tell Grandma it was your
invisible friend, your brother. Sneak
a spoonful of cream cheese icing
straight from the bowl
                   and lick your
fingers. Even the precise crunch
of a carrot stick is like an echo,
a short man at the back of a grainy

sepia-toned photo.

                  Turmeric Is Now™,
even though preliminary reports have
shown the detox capsules slowly
retoxify the body, rendering them as
carcinogenic as fresh tar.

                          But these
are preliminary findings, obviously,
and there are always other scientists
for hire. Eat your cinnamon-turmeric
capsules, kids, and get detoxified
right to the roots of your hair.

Fast Food Breakfast

The bagel he ordered had everything:
sesame seeds, nostalgia, onion powder,
regret, the memory of ice cream falling
slo-mo to sand. There were also pretty
redheads, 1893, booze, and two competing
theories on the origin of time, each of which
was about ⅔ correct.
                         The bagel was around
five inches across and always had a party
going, invited inventors like Tesla, Edison,
the ShamWow guy, and Stephanie.
The bagel assumed he already knew who
Stephanie was, that he'd mapped longitudes
for his least favourite destinations.
                                The bagel
had poppy seeds and hinted of garlic, but
it had also memorized Homer in the original
Greek and found schematics for the Pentagon
and West Edmonton Mall.
                          Even without the free
cream cheese, the Everything Bagel came with
much too much. He left it uneaten by the Timmy's
cash, missing the gentle thrill of paprika, but not
brave enough to know Good from Evil.
                                      Not yet.

Victimology, Redux

I could map her cartography
of bruises at once, even
pressed behind the one-way
glass at the 14th precinct
in a routine
                    victim line-up.
I relished my glimpse of her
and the others, some crying,
one retching, another with her
jeans-knee ripped and bloodied,
and wondered if I would get
the list of their names.
                              Mine
must have been a Beatrice —
she had that halo even trapped
in the 14th precinct, that quiet
catnip air of impregnable virtue.
I was that cat.
                    Get them to turn
right, I told the detective, and he
had a cattle prod to make them
obey. The one with the bloody
knee whimpered a bit, but my
eyes were for Beatrice, more
symbol than girl,
                    a clean Kleenex
that someone had sneezed in.
She was the one I hurt so perfect,
but I didn't tell the detective yet.
I'm so pleased the police keep

them caged like that,
                    with Miranda
rights as a bedtime story and one
good phone call home. But I knew
her bruises. *Let me see their left
sides,* I told the cop, *then have
them turn, super slow, toward me.*

The Great Reign

The dominant species on every
planet, including those a stupid
number of light-years away, has
always been
      Felis catus. Cats.
They form parliaments constructed
mostly of cheese to tempt in ever-
unsuspecting mice, who are woefully
oppressed by the global regime and
always have been.
                Always will be.
The official religion of high-ranking
politicians is worship of the Egyptian
cat goddess, Bast, though some
fringe believers in ancestral animism
remain:
      the cats who came before,
those to come. They bump noses
when they pass each other in
the street, and the rich refuse
to give handouts of kibble to alley
cats,
      strays, the Feral Cat Problem.
Society segments itself according
to breed. At the top are Persians
and Siamese, the have-nots largely
domestic shorthair.
            Most alpha cats
have a keen interest in marketing,
coupled with stock prices, freemium

businesses, and celebrity gossip
from edible milk-flavoured tabloids.
They have forever been the dominant
species, and live the lives that such
privilege affords.

        Even the alley cats,
even the Feral are all still *Felis catus*.
All still safe.

        But what's that smell, that whip
of a tail? A mouse. One mouse is weak,
defenceless, dinner. But what about two
mice? Thirteen thousand? #AllMice?

Gridlock

Stoplights only change once
every fortnight. Families in
minivans bring camping gear,
ham sandwiches to the first
intersection days in advance.
It's back-to-back
                   gridlock every block,
domestic squabbles simmering
in last-legs Miatas. If you turn,
it's fourteen days before
                   you can turn
again, or progress a bit more up
your chunk of potholed, potholed
road. Runners set up shop, delivering
Vietnamese takeout, cheap shoes,
even alcohol
                   if the fourteenth day is far off.
Everybody makes the same jokes
about leaps forward, immobile phones.
Sometimes people fall in
                   and out of love
with a person two or three cars behind,
and sometimes a person two or three
cars behind winds up with a windshield
wiper shoved up their bum. It's bedlam
for two weeks
                   every two weeks. But as the fourteenth
day draws nearer, the enmities and torrid
love affairs cease. Every car and SUV,
high-alert waiting.

Then: the green light,
first in fourteen days. Go! go! go! they all yell,
spurred on by their engines' great roar
into action. Some sputter, stall, but still
go on . . . and then the red light, the lurch
back to a standstill.
                    Go, say the traffic
lights, go at top speed, but stop just
a hair before you get what you need.

Happy

The last nihilists are so drunk
they don't even
                    matter. Laser
guns that years ago enhanced
all our fingertips shoot out
energy beams of pure mood,
and "mood" invariably means
"happy" or "calm."
                    We don't
have the mental fortitude for
war, or sex, or garish abstract
art with an angry blue slash

down the middle. None. Jobs,
now in fact filled in by sweet-
tempered robots who ask what
we long for, are replaced in
our own lives by an aimless
ambling without the philosophical
quagmires attached.
                    Every stock
price has swelled like an infection,
so of course each giddy non-nihilist
feels at last their time has come.

Tale of the Flood

It's always been raining and
agriculture's a myth: there have
never been proud yellow fields
of sunflowers.
        It's always been
raining and each house is on
stilts or else atop a garbage barge
adrift on one of several rivers:
Tigris, Euphrates, the impossible
Potomac.
        It's this wet everywhere,
but we can't ever swim because
of flesh-eating bacteria and, public
swimming pool-style, human pee.

Raining, always raining, a great
cumulonimbus ugly cry that feels
too private yet somehow encircles
the entire Earth.
        It's always been
flooded and we've always been
gathering artificial sunflowers to
bedeck the Ark, martialling every
species aboard.
        But knowing what
we know of lust, the crude trigonometry
of desire, does it not seem cruel
to only pick two of each kind?

Back, Back

Reverse. Somehow backwards
day became your backwards
life. The bluebirds who sang
in the blooming cherry tree
outside your window, when
forced to take back and swallow
their own birdsong, choke.
                          The tree
retracts its offering of fruits. You
find yourself shrinking more, more
each day. You mark your eight-inch
reduction in height with a notch
on the door frame,
                    which you have
to stand on the ceiling to tick off.
Yesterday was Grade 3. Today,
Grade 2. You study palindromes
all day and bring all the ingredients
for a sandwich for lunch, including
the raw onion which,
                      when you were
eight inches higher, your dad chopped
up combined with canned meat. You
feel like you're a tape rewinding except
that all the tracking's off, and although
it's Grade 3 you still remember doing
your taxes, driving stick shift, swaddling
your infant son.
                 The terror sets in: what if
you wake up and, having no years left

to relive, simply unwake and then that's
it for you? You thought these things in
Grade 3 Round 1 too.
                                    You've both always
thought them and can never think them.
Dad tucks you in bed and you try to hold
onto the palindromes
                        you learned in school:
We sew. Acrobats stab orca. You dream
a whole onion un-grows from the ground,
then you wake up and reverse again.

Acknowledgements

This book was written with the generous help of a Research and Creation grant from the Canada Council for the Arts.

Some of the poems in this collection first appeared elsewhere, including:

"Do The Sex" in *Impossible Archetype*

"Do Your Fucking Breathing Exercises" and "Let it Out" in *Room Magazine*

"Alt-Everything" and "*Republic 2*" in *The Antigonish Review*

"Gridlock" and "The Great Reign" in *Grain*

This book is also available as a Global Certified Accessible™ (GCA) ebook. ECW Press's ebooks are screen reader friendly and are built to meet the needs of those who are unable to read standard print due to blindness, low vision, dyslexia or a physical disability.

At ECW Press, we want you to enjoy our books in whatever format you like. If you've bought a print copy just send an email to ebook@ecwpress.com and include:

- the book title
- the name of the store where you purchased it
- a screenshot or picture of your order/receipt number and your name
- your preference of file type: PDF (for desktop reading), ePub (for a phone/tablet, Kobo, or Nook), mobi (for Kindle)

A real person will respond to your email with your ebook attached. Please note this offer is only for copies bought for personal use and does not apply to school or library copies.

Thank you for supporting an independently owned Canadian publisher with your purchase!

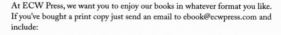